Nineteen Ways of Looking at Wang Wei

also by Eliot Weinberger
FROM NEW DIRECTIONS

Eliot Weinberger

*Nineteen Ways
of Looking at Wang Wei*

(with more ways)

Afterword by Octavio Paz

A NEW DIRECTIONS PAPERBOOK

Nineteen Ways of Looking at Wang Wei was first published by Moyer Bell Limited
in 1987. An earlier version first appeared in *Zero: Contemporary Buddhist Thought*,
edited by Eric Lerner. Paz's essay first appeared in *Vuelta* (Mexico City).
Reissued, with additional material, as New Directions Paperbook 1349 in 2016.
Manufactured in the United States of America.

Library of Congress Cataloging-in-Publication Data
Names: Weinberger, Eliot, author. | Paz, Octavio, 1914–1998, writer of afterword.
Title: 19 ways of looking at Wang Wei : with more ways / Eliot Weinberger ;
afterword by Octavio Paz.
Other titles: Nineteen ways of looking at Wang Wei.
Description: New York, NY : New Directions Books, 2016.
Identifiers: LCCN 2016021270 | ISBN 9780811226202 (acid-free paper)
Subjects: LCSH: Wang, Wei, 701–761. Lu chai. |
Wang, Wei, 701–761—Translations—History and criticism. |
Chinese language—Translating. | Poetry—Translating.
Classification: LCC PL2676.A683 W43 2016 | DDC 895.11/3—dc23
LC record available at https://lccn.loc.gov/2016021270

6 8 9 7

New Directions Books are published for James Laughlin
by New Directions Publishing Corporation
80 Eighth Avenue, New York 10011

CONTENTS

NINETEEN WAYS OF
LOOKING AT WANG WEI

Poetry is that which is worth translating.

For example, this four-line poem, 1200 years old: a mountain, a forest, the setting sun illuminating a patch of moss. It is a scrap of literary Chinese, no longer even pronounced as its writer would have spoken it. It is a thing, forever itself, inseparable from its language.

And yet something about it has caused it to lead a nomadic life: insinuating itself in the minds of readers, demanding understanding — but always on the reader's own terms — provoking thought, sometimes compelling writing in other languages. Great poetry lives in a state of perpetual transformation, perpetual translation: the poem dies when it has no place to go.

The transformations that take shape in print — and not in the minds of readers — that take the formal name of "translation," become their own beings, set out on their own wanderings. Some live long and some don't. What kind of creatures are they? What happens when a poem, once Chinese and still Chinese, becomes a piece of English, Spanish, French poetry?

1

(text)

鹿柴
空山不見人,
但聞人語響.
返景入深林,
復照青苔上

The poem is by Wang Wei (c. 700–761), known in his life-time as a wealthy Buddhist painter and calligrapher, and to later generations as a master poet in an age of masters, the Tang Dynasty. The quatrain is from a series of twenty poems on various sights near the Wang (no relation) River. The poems were written as part of a massive horizontal landscape scroll, a genre he invented. The painting was copied (translated) for centuries. The original is lost, and the earliest surviving copy comes from the 17th century: Wang's landscape after 900 years of transformation.

In classical Chinese, each character (ideogram) represents a word of a single syllable. Few of the characters are, as is commonly thought, entirely representational.

But some of the basic vocabulary is indeed pictographic, and with those few hundred characters one can play the game of pretending to read Chinese.

Reading the poem left to right, top to bottom, the second character in line 1 is apparently a *mountain*; the last character in the same line a *person*—both are stylizations that evolved from more literal representations. Character 4 in line 1 was a favorite of Ezra Pound's: what he interpreted as an eye on legs; that is, the eye in motion, *to see*. Character 5 in line 3 is two trees, *forest*. Spatial relationships are concretely portrayed in character 3 of line 3, *to enter*, and character 5 of line 4, *above* or *on (top of)*.

More typical of Chinese is character 2 of line 4, *to shine*, which contains an image of the sun in the upper left and of fire at the bottom, as well as a purely phonetic element—key to the word's pronunciation—in the upper right. Most of the other characters have no pictorial content useful for decipherment.

2

(transliteration)

Lù zhái

Kōng shān bù jián rén
Dàn wén rén yǔ xiǎng
Fǎn jǐng (yǐng) ru shēn lín
Fù zhào qīng tái shàng

The transliteration is from modern Chinese, using the current, quirky *pinyin* system. Obvious, perhaps, to the Romanians who helped develop it, but not to English speakers, is that the *zh* is a *j* sound, the *x* a heavily aspirated *s*, and the *q* a hard *ch*. The *a* is the *ah* of *father*.

Though the characters have remained the same, their pronunciation has changed considerably since the Tang Dynasty. In the 1920s the philologist Bernhard Karlgren attempted to recreate Tang speech; a transliteration of this poem, using Karlgren's system, may be found in Hugh M. Stimson's *55 Tang Poems*. Unfortunately, the transliteration is written in its own forbidding language, with upside-down letters, letters floating above the words, and a leveled forest of diacritical marks.

Chinese has the least number of sounds of any major language. In modern Chinese a monosyllable is pronounced in one of four tones, but any given sound in any given tone has scores of possible meanings. Thus a Chinese monosyllabic word (and often the written character) is comprehensible only in the context of the phrase: a linguistic basis, perhaps, for Chinese philosophy, which was always based on relation rather than substance.

For poetry, this means that rhyme is inevitable, and Western "meter" impossible. Chinese prosody is largely concerned with the number of characters per line and the arrangement of tones — both of which are untranslatable. But translators tend to rush in where wise men never tread, and often may be seen attempting to nurture Chinese rhyme patterns in the hostile environment of a Western language.

3

(character-by-character translation)

1. Empty	mountain(s) hill(s)	(negative)	to see	person people
2. But	to hear	person people	words conversation	sound to echo
3. To return	bright(ness) shadow(s)*	to enter	deep	forest
4. To return Again	to shine to reflect	green blue black	moss lichen	above on (top of) top

I have presented only those definitions that are possible for this text. There are others.

A single character may be noun, verb, and adjective. It may even have contradictory readings: character 2 of line 3 is either *jing* (brightness) or *ying* (shadow). Again, context is all. Of particular difficulty to the Western translator is the absence of tense in Chinese verbs: in the poem, what is happening has happened and will happen. Similarly, nouns have no number: rose is a rose is all roses.

---

* According to François Cheng, *returning shadows* is a trope meaning rays of sunset.

Contrary to the evidence of most translations, the first-person singular rarely appears in Chinese poetry. By eliminating the controlling individual mind of the poet, the experience becomes both universal and immediate to the reader.

The title of the poem, *Lu zhai*, is a place-name, something like *Deer Grove*, which I take from a map of Illinois. It probably alludes to the Deer Park in Sarnath, where the Gautama Buddha preached his first sermon.

The first two lines are fairly straightforward. The second couplet has, as we shall see, quite a few possible readings, all of them equally "correct."

4

The Form of the Deer

So lone seem the hills; there is no one in sight there.
But whence is the echo of voices I hear?
The rays of the sunset pierce slanting the forest,
And in their reflection green mosses appear.

—W.J.B. FLETCHER, 1919
(Fletcher, *Gems of Chinese Verse*)

The translation is typical of those written before the general recognition of Ezra Pound's *Cathay*, first published in 1915. Pound's small book, containing some of the most beautiful poems in the English language, was based on a notebook of literal Chinese translations prepared by the orientalist Ernest Fenollosa and a Japanese informant. The "accuracy" of Pound's versions remains a sore point: pedants still snort at the errors, but Wai-lim Yip has demonstrated that Pound, who at the time knew no Chinese, intuitively corrected mistakes in the Fenollosa manuscript. Regardless of its scholarly worth, *Cathay* marked, in T. S. Eliot's words, "the invention of Chinese poetry in our time." Rather than stuffing the original into the corset of traditional verse forms, as Fletcher and many others had done, Pound created a new poetry in English drawn from what he found was unique to the Chinese.

"Every force," said Mother Ann Lee of the Shakers, "evolves a form." Pound's genius was the discovery of the living matter, the force, of the Chinese poem — what he called the "news that stays news" through the centuries. This living matter functions somewhat like DNA, spinning out individual translations that are relatives, not clones, of the original. The relationship between original and translation is parent-child. And there are, inescapably, some translations that are overly attached to their originals, and others that are constantly rebelling.

Fletcher, like all early (and many later) translators, feels he must explain and "improve" the original poem. Where Wang's sunlight *enters* the forest, Fletcher's rays *pierce slanting*; where Wang states simply that voices are heard, Fletcher invents a first-person narrator who asks where the sounds are coming from. (And if the hills are *there*, where is the narrator?)

In line 4, ambiguity has been translated into confusion: Fletcher's line has no meaning. (What reflection where?) Or perhaps the line has a lovely and unlikely Platonic subtlety: if *their* refers to the mosses, then what *appears* is the reflection of moss itself.

Fletcher explains his curious (and equally Platonic) title with a note that *zhai* means "the place where the deer sleeps, its 'form.' "

5

Deer-Park Hermitage

There seems to be no one on the empty mountain . . .
And yet I think I hear a voice,
Where sunlight, entering a grove,
Shines back to me from the green moss.

—WITTER BYNNER & KIANG KANG-HU, 1929
(Bynner & Kiang, *The Jade Mountain*)

Witter Bynner was a primary purveyor of Chinoiserie translation in English in the 1920s — though not as extreme an exoticist as his Imagist counterparts Amy Lowell and Florence Ayscough, who never translated this poem. His Chinese poet does, however, write from the ethereal mists of tentative half-perception: *there seems to be, and yet I think I hear.* (Wang, however, quite plainly sees no one and hears someone.)

Where Wang is specific, Bynner's Wang seems to be watching the world through a haze of opium reflected in a hundred thimbles of wine. It is a world where no statement can be made without a pregnant, sensitive, world-weary ellipsis. The *I* even hears a voice where the sunlight shines back to him from the moss. Such lack of sense was traditionally explained by reference to the mystical, inscrutable Fu Manchu East.

6

The Deer Park

An empty hill, and no one in sight
But I hear the echo of voices.
The slanting sun at evening penetrates the deep woods
And shines reflected on the blue lichens.

— SOAME JENYNS, 1944
(Jenyns, *Further Poems of the T'ang Dynasty*)

Dull, but fairly direct, Jenyns's only additions are the inevitable *I* and the explanatory *slanting* sun *at evening*. He is the only translator to prefer lichen to moss, though in plural form the word is particularly ugly.

In the fourth line *zhao* becomes both *shines reflected*, rather than one or the other, but he is still in the "reflected" trap: from what is the sun reflected?

Chinese poetry was based on the precise observation of the physical world. Jenyns and other translators come from a tradition where the notion of verifying a poetic image would be silly, where the word "poetic" itself is synonymous with "dreamy."

He might have squeaked by had he written *And shines reflected by the blue lichens* — accurate to nature, if not to Wang. But Jenyns — at the time Assistant Keeper of the Department of Oriental Antiquities at the British

Museum, translating through the Blitz—was so far re-moved from the poem's experience that he found it nec-essary to add the following footnote to line 2: "The woods are so thick that woodcutters and herdsmen are hidden."

7

La Forêt

Dans la montagne tout est solitaire,
On entend de bien loin l'écho des voix humaines,
Le soleil qui pénètre au fond de la forêt
Reflète son éclat sur la mousse vert.

— G. MARGOULIES, 1948
(Margouliès, *Anthologie raisonée de la littérature Chinoise*)

[*The Forest*. On the mountain everything is solitary, / One hears from far off the echo of human voices, / The sun that penetrates to the depths of the forest / Reflects its ray on the green moss.]

Margoulies prefers to generalize Wang's specifics: *Deer Grove* becomes, simply, *The Forest*; *nobody in sight* becomes the ponderous malaise of *everything is solitary*. In the second line he poeticizes the voices by having them come from *far off*. The French indefinite pronoun happily excludes the need for a narrator.

8

Deer Forest Hermitage

Through the deep wood, the slanting sunlight
Casts motley patterns on the jade-green mosses.
No glimpse of man in this lonely mountain,
Yet faint voices drift on the air.

— CHANG YIN-NAN
& LEWIS C. WALMSLEY, 1958
(Wang Wei, *Poems*, trans. Chang & Walmsley)

Chang and Walmsley published the first book-length translation of Wang Wei in English, but unfortunately their work bore little resemblance to the original.

In this poem, the couplets are reversed for no reason. The voices are *faint* and *drift on the air*. The mountain is *lonely* (a Western conceit, inimical to Wang's Buddhism, that empty = lonely) but it's a decorator's delight: the moss is as green as jade and the sunlight casts *motley patterns*.

It is a classic example of the translator attempting to "improve" the original. Such cases are not uncommon, and are the product of a kind of unspoken contempt for the foreign poet. It never occurs to Chang and Walmsley that Wang could have written the equivalent of *casts motley patterns on the jade-green mosses* had he wanted to. He didn't.

In its way a spiritual exercise, translation is dependent on the dissolution of the translator's ego: an absolute humility toward the text. A bad translation is the insistent voice of the translator — that is, when one sees no poet and hears only the translator speaking.

9

The Deer Enclosure

On the lonely mountain
I meet no one,
I hear only the echo
of human voices.
At an angle the sun's rays
enter the depths of the wood,
And shine
upon the green moss.

— C. J. CHEN & MICHAEL BULLOCK, 1960
(Chen & Bullock, *Poems of Solitude*)

Chen and Bullock make some now familiar "improvements": the first-person narrator, the *lonely* mountain, the sun at *an angle*. Wang's *see* becomes *meet* in their second line; there's a difference. Their main innovation is the creation of eight lines for Wang's four—a gesture that apparently caught them short when they had to break the last line into two.

10

On the empty mountains no one can be seen,
But human voices are heard to resound.
The reflected sunlight pierces the deep forest
And falls again upon the mossy ground.

> — JAMES J. Y. LIU, 1962
> (Liu, *The Art of Chinese Poetry*)

Liu's book applied the techniques of 1940s New Criticism to the interpretation of Chinese poetry. The New Critics preached a strict ahistorical and nonbiographical attention to sense in the poem, and especially appreciated ambiguities, ironies, elaborate metaphors, and learned allusions. They generally neglected music. Thus Liu's version is more accurate than most, but the first two lines heave, the third gasps, and the fourth falls with a thud on the rhyming mossy ground.

In his commentary, after translating the first line literally as *Empty mountain not see people*, Liu writes:

> The poet simply says "not see people," not "I do not see anyone" or even "One does not see anyone": consequently no awkward questions such as "If no one is here, who is hearing the voices" or "If you are here, how can the mountains be said to be empty?" will occur to the reader.

(Logicians can work on that one.) He continues:

> Instead, he is made to feel the presence of Nature as
> a whole, in which the mountains, the human voices,
> the sunlight, the mosses, are all equals. To preserve
> this sense of impersonality in English, one has to
> resort to the "passive voice": *On the empty mountains
> no one can be seen.*

But, by changing the expected *is* to *can be* in the first line,
Liu has transformed Wang's specifics into a general and
slightly pompous remark: "In an empty room no furni-
ture can be seen." The redundant *human voices* is an in-
congruous allusion to T. S. Eliot ("human voices wake
us and we drown") and the 19th century *resound* is only
there to rhyme with *ground*. A ray of sunlight might *pierce*
the deep forest, but *reflected sunlight* wouldn't, and absent
from Liu's third line is the sense that it is late afternoon,
that the sunlight is returning to the forest. In the fourth
line, *green* has been subtracted, *ground* added. In Liu's
favor, however, are the absence of the "I" and the usual
explanations.

11

Deep in the Mountain Wilderness

Deep in the mountain wilderness
Where nobody ever comes
Only once in a great while
Something like the sound of a far off voice,
The low rays of the sun
Slip through the dark forest,
And gleam again on the shadowy moss.

— KENNETH REXROTH, 1970
(Rexroth, *Love and the Turning Year*)

The taxonomy of Chinese translators is fairly simple. There are the Sinologists, most of whom are incapable of writing poetry, because they know everything about the original language and not much about the language into which they're translating. The few exceptions, such as Burton Watson and Arthur Waley, were well-read in — and part of the community of — contemporary English-language poetry. Then there are the poets: most know no Chinese, a few know some. Kenneth Rexroth belonged to this last category (along with Gary Snyder and the later Pound) — although this particular example is perhaps more "imitation" than translation.

Rexroth ignores what he presumably dislikes, or feels cannot be translated, in the original. The title is eliminated, and the philosophical *empty mountain* becomes the empirical *mountain wilderness*. Certain words and phrases are his own invention. One of them, *where nobody ever comes* leads him into a trap: he must modify *the sound of a far off voice* with *something like*, and it makes a rather klutzy fourth line. But this is clearly the first real poem of the group, able to stand by itself. It is the closest to the spirit, though not the letter, of the original: the poem Wang might have written had he been born a 20th-century American.

Rexroth's great skill is apparent in three tiny gestures. In line 2, by using *comes* rather than the more obvious *goes* he has created an implicit narrator-observer (i.e., "comes here where I am") without using the first person. Second, he takes an utterly ordinary phrase, *once in a great while*, and lets us hear it, for the first time, as something lovely and onomatopoeic. And third, Rexroth's *slip* for Wang's *enter* is perhaps too sensual—reminiscent of Sanskrit forest trysts—but it is irresistible.

12

Deer Fence

Empty hills, no one in sight,
only the sound of someone talking;
late sunlight enters the deep wood,
shining over the green moss again.

— BURTON WATSON, 1971
(Watson, *Chinese Lyricism*)

Watson is a prolific and particularly fine translator of classical Chinese poetry, history, and philosophy; he is comparable in this century only to Arthur Waley, who unfortunately never translated this poem. He is also the first scholar whose work displays an affinity with the modernist revolution in American poetry: absolute precision, concision, and the use of everyday speech.

[Curiously, while most of the French and American modernists lit joss sticks at the altars of their newfound Chinese ancestors, the scholars of Chinese ignored, or were actively hostile to modern poetry. Many still are. Chinese poets were, however, excited by the doings in the West. Hu Shih's 1917 manifestoes, which launched the "Chinese Renaissance" in literature by rejecting classical language and themes in favor of vernacular and "realism", were largely inspired by Ezra Pound's 1913 Imagist manifestoes. Full circle: Pound thought he found it in China, Hu Shih thought it came from the West.]

Watson here renders the first two characters of line 1 with two words: no article, no explanation. His presentation of the image is as direct as the Chinese. There are 24 English words (six per line) for the Chinese 20, yet every word of the Chinese has been translated without indulging, as others have done, in a telegraphic minimalism. In the translation of Chinese poetry, as in everything, nothing is more difficult than simplicity.

More than arrangements of tones, rhymes, and number of characters per line, Chinese poetry, like all ancient poetries, is based on parallelism: the dual (yin-yang) nature of the universe. Wang's first two lines are typical: *see no people / but hear people.* He even repeats the character for *people.* Watson retains Wang's parallelism effortlessly enough *(no one / someone)* yet he is the first translator to do so.

Watson prefers *hills* to *mountains* and *Fence* in the title to *Park* or *Enclosure.* This may be because, in Wang's painted scroll, the landscape is more hilly than mountainous and the deer are indeed enclosed by a fence.

13

Deer Enclosure

Empty mountain: no man is seen,
But voices of men are heard.
Sun's reflection reaches into the woods
And shines upon the green moss.

— WAI-LIM YIP, 1972
(Wang Wei, *Hiding the Universe*, trans. Yip)

Yip is a critic who has written brilliantly on the importance of Chinese poetics to 20th-century American poetry. As a translator he is less successful, perhaps because English is apparently his second language. (It is rarely possible, though many try, to translate out of one's natural language.) Thus the strangeness of *no man is seen* and the oddly anthropomorphic *reaches into*.

Like Burton Watson (#12), Yip follows Wang's repetition of *person* in the first two lines (though his *persons* are *men*) and presents six English words per line for the Chinese five. But unlike Watson and the other translators, Yip actually gives us less than the original — leaving out *deep* and *again*.

In a later version of this translation, published in his anthology *Chinese Poetry*, Yip clipped the first line to the almost pidgin *Empty mountain: no man.*

14

Deer Park

Hills empty, no one to be seen
We hear only voices echoed —
With light coming back into the deep wood
The top of the green moss is lit again.

— G. W. ROBINSON, 1973
(Robinson, *Poems of Wang Wei*)

Robinson's translation, published by Penguin Books, is, unhappily, the most widely available edition of Wang in English.

In this poem Robinson not only creates a narrator, he makes it a group, as though it were a family outing. With that one word, *we*, he effectively scuttles the mood of the poem.

Reading the last word of the poem as *top*, he offers an image that makes little sense on the forest floor: one would have to be small indeed to think of moss vertically.

For a jolt to the system, try reading this aloud.

15

En la Ermita del Parque de los Venados

> No se ve gente en este monte.
> Sólo se oyen, lejos, voces.
> Por los ramajes la luz rompe.
> Tendida entre la yerba brilla verde.

> — OCTAVIO PAZ,
> (Paz, *Versiones y Diversiones*)

[*In the Deer Park Hermitage.* No people are seen on this mountain. / Only voices, far off, are heard. / Light breaks through the branches. / Spread among the grass it shines green.]

In the second edition of *Versiones y Diversiones*, his selected translations, Paz wrote:

The translation of this poem is particularly difficult, for the poem carries to an extreme the characteristics of Chinese poetry: universality, impersonality, absence of time, absence of subject. In Wang Wei's poem, the solitude of the mountain is so great that not even the poet himself is present. After a number of attempts I wrote these four unrhymed lines: three with nine syllables each and the last with eleven.

Months later, reading some Mahayana texts, I was surprised by the frequency with which the Western paradise, domain of the Amida Buddha, is mentioned. I remembered that Wang Wei had been a fervent Buddhist: I consulted one of his biographies and discovered that his devotion for Amida was such that he had written a hymn in which he speaks of his desire to be reborn in the Western Paradise — the place of the setting sun . . .

This is nature poetry, but a Buddhist nature poetry: Does not the quatrain reflect, even more than the naturalistic aestheticism traditional in this kind of composition, a spiritual experience? Sometime later, Burton Watson, who knows my love for Chinese poetry, sent me his *Chinese Lyricism*. There I encountered a confirmation of my suspicion: for Wang Wei the light of the setting sun had a very precise meaning. An allusion to the Amida Buddha: At the end of the afternoon the adept meditates and, like the moss in the forest, receives illumination. Poetry perfectly objective, impersonal, far from the mysticism of a St. John of the Cross, but no less authentic or profound than that of the Spanish poet. Transformation of man and nature before the divine light, although in a sense inverse to that of Western tradition. In place of the humanization of the world that surrounds us, the Oriental spirit is impregnated with the objectivity, passivity and impersonality of the trees, grass and rocks, so that, impersonally, it receives the impartial light of a revelation that is also impersonal. Without losing the reality of the trees, rocks, and earth, Wang Wei's mountain and forest are emblems of the void. Imitating his reticence, I limited myself to lightly changing the last two lines:

> No se ve gente en este monte.
> Solo se oyen, lejos, voces.
> La luz poniente rompe entre las ramas.
> En la yerba tendida brilla verde.

[No people are seen on this mountain. / Only voices, far off, are heard. / Western light breaks through the branches. / Spread over the grass it shines green.]

Paz drops *empty* from the first line; in the second, like Margouliès (#7) and Rexroth (#11), he makes the voices *far off*. His third line, though not strictly literal, may be the most beautiful of all the versions: replacing the abstract *light enters the forest* with the concrete and dramatic *light breaks through the branches* — the light almost becoming the sudden illumination, *satori* of Wang's Chan (Zen) Buddhism. In the fourth line, the *moss* has become *grass*, no doubt because the Spanish word for moss, *musgo*, is unpleasantly squishy. (How mossy — soft and damp — is the English *moss!*)

What is missing from these lovely third and fourth lines is the cyclical quality of the original. Wang begins both lines with *to return*: taking a specific time of day and transforming it into a moment, frozen in its recurrence, that becomes cosmic. Reading the image as a metaphor for illumination, the ordinary (sunset in the forest) represents the extraordinary (the enlightenment of the individual) which, in terms of the cosmos, is as ordinary as sunlight illuminating a patch of moss.

An endless series of negations: The mountain seems *empty* (without people) because no one's in sight. But people are heard, so the mountain is not *empty*. But the mountain is *empty* because it is an illusion. The light from the Western Paradise, the light called *shadow* falls.

[See Paz's afterword for his third version of the poem.]

16

Li Ch'ai

In empty mountains no one can be seen.
But here might echoing voices cross.
Reflecting rays
entering the deep wood
Glitter again
on the dark green moss.

—WILLIAM McNAUGHTON, 1974
(McNaughton, *Chinese Literature*)

McNaughton offers the Chinese place-name as a title, but his transliteration is incorrect — something like *Beer Park*.

Line 1 copies James Liu (#10) by placing it in the passive voice and, like Liu, seems almost a parody of Eastern Wisdom. Line 2 places the action *here* for no reason and adds *cross* for the rhyme scheme he has imposed on himself. (Not much rhymes with *moss*; it's something of an albatross.) The conditional *might* is bizarre. (Well, do they or don't they?)

Splitting the last couplet into four lines is apparently an attempt at pictorial representation.

17

Clos aux cerfs

Montagne déserte. Personne n'est en vue.
Seuls, les échos des voix résonnent, au loin.
Ombres retournent dans la forêt profonde :
Dernier éclat de la mousse, vert.

— FRANÇOIS CHENG, 1977
(Cheng, *L'écriture poétique chinoise.*
In English: *Chinese Poetic Writing*, trans.
Donald A. Riggs & Jerome P. Seaton.)

[*Deer Enclosure*. Deserted mountain. No one in sight. / Only, the echoes of voices resound, far off. / Shadows return to the deep forest: / Last gleaming of the moss, green.]

Cheng writes, as translated by Riggs:

[Wang] describes here a walk on the mountain, which is at the same time a spiritual experience, an experience of the Void and of communion with Nature. The first couplet should be interpreted "On the empty mountain I meet no one; only some echoes of voices of people walking come to me." But through the suppression of the personal pronoun and of locative elements the poet identifies himself immediately with the "empty mountain," which is therefore no longer merely a "complement of place"; similarly, in the third line he *is* the ray of the setting sun that penetrates the forest. From the point of view of content, the first two lines present the poet as still "not seeing"; in his ears the echoes of human voices still resound. The last two lines are centered in the theme of "vision": to see the golden effect of the setting sun on the green moss. Seeing here signifies illumination and deep communion with the essence of things. Elsewhere the poet often omits the personal pronoun to effect the description of *actions in sequence* where human acts are related to movements in nature.

Cheng also presents a literal translation of the poem:

> Montagne vide / ne percevoir personne
> Seulement entendre / voix humaine résonner
> Ombre-retournée / penetrer forêt profonde
> Encore luire / sur la mousse verte

It is curious to see how Cheng poeticizes and even Westernizes his literal version to create a finished translation. The Buddhist *montagne vide* (empty mountain) becomes the Romantic *montagne déserte* (deserted mountain). *Échos* and *au loin* (far off) are added to the second line. In the third, his literal *ombre-retournée* (returned shadow — a trope he notes as meaning "rays of sunset") has become a subject and verb, *ombres retournent* (shadows return) which considerably alters the meaning. Cheng's last line is quite peculiar: the literal *Encore luire sur la mousse verte* (to shine again on the green moss) becomes *Dernier eclat de la mousse, vert* (last gleaming of the moss, green — the green referring to the gleaming, not the moss). The line owes more to French Symbolists than to Tang Buddhists.

Translations aside, Cheng's book is a luminous, original study of Chinese poetry. In the English version, first published in 1982, Jerome P. Seaton, working "after the interpretations of" Cheng, offers a translation that seems to owe more to Gary Snyder's 1978 poem (#19) than to Cheng:

Deer Park

Empty mountain. None to be seen.
But hear, the echoing of voices.
Returning shadows enter deep, the grove.
Sun shines, again, on lichen's green.

18

The Deer Park

Not the shadow on a man on the deserted hill —
And yet one hears voices speaking;
Deep in the seclusion of the woods,
Stray shafts of the sun pick out the green moss.

— H. C. CHANG, 1977
(Chang, *Chinese Literature, Vol II: Nature Poetry*)

Chang translates 12 of Wang's 20 words, and makes up the rest.

In line 1 the first *on* is probably a typographical error, but in such surroundings it's hard to tell. In any event, what's that *shadow* doing (or more exactly, not doing) there? Only the shadow knows.

Why are the *shafts* of sun *stray*? Why are they *shafts* at all? And why do they *pick out* the moss? The verb is unavoidably reminiscent of the consumption of winkles and crab.

In short, the poem is more Chang than Wang. (It is taken from a three-volume set, all by the same translator, and published, oddly, by Columbia University Press.)

19

Empty mountains:
>   no one to be seen.
Yet—hear—
>   human sounds and echoes.
Returning sunlight
>   enters the dark woods;
Again shining
>   on the green moss, above.

>   — GARY SNYDER, 1978
>   *(Journal for the Protection of All Beings*, No. 4, Fall 1978.
>   Reprinted in *The Gary Snyder Reader)*

Surely one of the best translations, partially because of Snyder's lifelong forest experience. Like Rexroth (#11), he can *see* the scene. Every word of Wang has been translated, and nothing added, yet the translation exists as an American poem.

Changing the passive *is heard* to the imperative *hear* is particularly beautiful, and, though unlikely, is not strictly incorrect: it creates an exact moment, which is now. Giving us both meanings, *sounds and echoes*, for the last word of line 2 is, like most sensible ideas, revolutionary. Translators usually assume that only one reading of a foreign word or phrase may be presented, despite the fact that perfect correspondence is rare.

The poem ends strangely. Snyder takes the last word, which everyone else has read as *on*, and translates it with its alternative meaning, *above*, isolating it from the phrase with a comma. What's going on? Moss presumably is only above if one is a rock or bug. Or are we meant to look up, after seeing the moss, back toward the sun: the vertical metaphor of enlightenment?

In answer to my query, Snyder wrote: "The reason for '. . . moss, above' . . . is that the sun is entering (in its sunset sloping, hence 'again'—a final shaft) the woods, and illuminating some moss *up in the trees*. (NOT ON ROCKS.) This is how my teacher Ch'en Shih-hsiang saw it, and my wife (Japanese) too, the first time she looked at the poem."

The point is that translation is more than a leap from dictionary to dictionary; it is a reimagining of the poem. As such, every reading of every poem, regardless of language, is an act of translation: translation into the reader's intellectual and emotional life. As no individual reader remains the same, each reading becomes a different—not merely another—reading. The same poem cannot be read twice.

Snyder's explanation is only one moment, the latest, when the poem suddenly transforms before our eyes. Wang's twenty characters remain the same, but the poem continues in a state of restless change.

[1979]

AFTERWORD

Eliot Weinberger's essay on the successive translations of Wang Wei's little poem illustrates, with succinct clarity, not only the evolution of the art of translation in the modern period but at the same time the changes in poetic sensibility. His examples come from English and, to a lesser extent, from French; I am sure that a parallel exploration of German or Italian would produce similar results. Weinberger cites only one Spanish version, my own. There may be another, and perhaps one or two in Portuguese. One must admit, however, that Spanish and Portuguese do not enjoy a *corpus* of Chinese translation similar in importance or quality to that of other languages. This is regrettable: the modern era has discovered other classicisms besides that of Greco-Roman culture, and one of them is China and Japan.

Weinberger's essay led me back to my own translation. Probably the greatest difficulty for any translator of a Chinese poem is the unique temper of the language and of the writing. The majority of the poems in the *Shi-jing*, the most ancient collection of Chinese poetry, are written in lines of four syllables that are four characters / words. For example, the phonetic transcription of the first line of a small erotic poem in the *Shi-jing* is composed of these four monosyllables: *Xing nu qi shu*. The literal translation is: *Sweet girl how pretty*. It is not impossible to transform this phrase into a line from a ballad: *¡Qué linda la dulce niña!* or *How lovely the pretty maiden!* Five words and eight syllables, twice the original. Arthur Waley thought to resolve the prosodic problem by having each Chinese monosyllable correspond to a tonic accent in the English line. The result was English lines that were quite long, but with the same number of accents as the Chinese original. This method, besides being not terribly perfect, is inapplicable in Spanish: in our language words generally have more syllables than English and less tonic accents. The equivalent of our hendecasyllable is the English iambic pentameter. Our line has either three accents (in the fourth syllable, in the seventh or eighth, and in the tenth) or only two (in the sixth and the tenth). In contrast, the English line has five accents or rhythmic beats. Furthermore, in English the number of syllables may vary; in Spanish it is fixed. As for rhyme, Spanish is more fortunate than English: not only do we have more consonants, but we may also rely on a rich assonance. The great advantage of the assonant is that the rhyme becomes a distant echo, one which never exactly repeats the ending of the previous line. I will note, finally, a small similarity between Chinese and Spanish versification: in Chinese poetry only paired verses are rhymed, exactly like our *romances* and traditional assonant poems.

The first to attempt to make English poems out of Chinese originals was Ezra Pound. All of us since who have translated Chinese and Japanese poetry are not only his followers but his debtors. I never found Pound's theory of translating Chinese persuasive, and in other writings I have tried to explain my reasons. It doesn't matter: though his theories seemed unreliable, his practice not only convinced me but, literally, enchanted me. Pound did not attempt to find metrical equivalents or rhymes: taking off from the images-ideograms of the originals, he wrote English poems in free verse. Those poems had (and still have) an enormous poetic freshness; at the same time they allow us to glimpse another civilization, and one quite distant from Western Greco-Roman tradition.

The poems of *Cathay* (1915) were written in an energetic language and in irregular verses which I have rather loosely labeled as free. In fact, although they do not have fixed measures, each one of them is a verbal unity. Nothing could be more remote from the prose chopped into short lines that today passes for free verse. Do Pound's poems correspond to the originals? A useless question: Pound *invented*, as Eliot said, Chinese poetry in English. The points of departure were some ancient Chinese poems, revived and changed by a great poet; the result was other poems. Others: the same. With that small volume of translations Pound, to a great extent, began modern poetry in English. Yet, at the same time, he also began something unique: the modern tradition of classical Chinese poetry in the poetic conscience of the West.

Pound's effort was a success, and after *Cathay* many others followed on various paths. I am thinking above all of Arthur Waley. The translations of Chinese and Japanese poetry into English have been so great and so diverse that they themselves form a chapter in the modern poetry of the language. I find nothing similar in French, although there are notable translations, such as those by Claude Roy or François Cheng. Certainly we owe to Claudel, Segalen, and Saint-John Perse poetic visions of China — but not memorable translations. It's a pity. In Spanish this lack has impoverished us.

In my own isolated attempts I followed, at first, the examples of Pound and, more than anyone, Waley — a ductile talent, but one less intense and less powerful. Later, little by little, I found my own way. At the beginning I used free verse; later I tried to adjust myself to a fixed rule, without of course attempting to reproduce Chinese meter. In general, I have endeavored to retain the number of lines of each poem, not to scorn assonances and to respect, as much as possible, the parallelism. This last element is central to Chinese poetry, but neither Pound nor Waley gave it the attention it deserves. Nor do the other translators in English. It is a serious omission not only because parallelism is the nucleus of the best Chinese poems but also because it corresponds to the vision of the universe of the Chinese poets and philosophers: the *yin* and the *yang*. The unity that splits into duality to reunite and to divide again. I would add that parallelism links, however slightly, our own indigenous Mexican poetry with that of China.

In the Han era they moved from a four-syllable line to one of five and seven (*gu shi*). These poems are composed in a strict tonal counterpoint. (The classical language has four tones.) The number of lines is undefined and only paired lines are rhymed. During the Tang period versification became more more strict and they wrote poems of eight and four lines (*lushi* and *jueju*, respectively). The lines of those poems are, as in the earlier style, composed of five and seven syllables; the same rhyme is used throughout the poem. The other rules apply to parallelism (the four lines in the center of the poem must form two antithetical couplets) and the tonal structure. This last recalls, in certain respects, classical quantitative versification — although the rhythm does not come from the combination of short and long syllables but rather from the alternation of tones. Every Chinese poem offers a true counterpoint that cannot be reproduced in any Indo-European language. I will spare the reader the chart of the various combinations (two for the five syllable lines and two for the seven). There are other forms: the *ci* (*tz'u*), poetry written to accompany already existing musical tunes and with lines of unequal length; dramatic verse (*ju*) and the lyric-dramatic (*sanju*).

Wang Wei's poem is written in four lines of five syllables each (*jueju*); the second line rhymes with the fourth. In order to transmit the information of the original, while attempting to recreate the poem in Spanish, I decided to use a line of nine syllables. I chose this meter not only because of its greater amplitude but also because it appeared to be, without actually being, a truncated hendecasyllable. It is the least traditional of our meters and it appears infrequently in Spanish poetry, except among the "modernists" — above all, Rubén Darío — who used it a great deal. I also decided to use assonant rhyme, but unlike the Chinese original I rhymed all four lines. The poem is divided into two parts. The first alludes to the solitude of the forest, and aural rather than visual sensations predominate (no one is seen, only voices are heard). The second refers to the apparition of light in a forest clearing and is composed of silently visual sensations: the light breaks through the branches, falls on the moss, and, in a manner of speaking, rises again. Attentive to this sensual and spiritual division, I divided the poem into two pairs: the first line rhymes with the second and the third rhymes with the fourth. I left the two first lines of my earlier version intact, but I radically changed the third and the fourth lines:

> No se ve gente en este monte,
> sólo se oyen, lejos, voces.
> Bosque profundo. Luz poniente:
> alumbra el musgo y, verde, asciende.

[No people are seen on this mountain, / only voices, far-off, are heard. / Deep forest. Western light: / it illuminates the moss and, green, rises.]

The first two lines need no explanation. It seems to me that I succeeded in transmitting the information while conserving the impersonality of the original: the "I" is implicit. The third line, according to François Cheng, means literally: *returning shadow — to penetrate — deep — forest.* Cheng points out that *returning shadow* alludes to the western sun. James J. Y. Liu translates in similar terms but, with greater propriety, says *reflected light* in place of *returning shadow*. In his literary version Liu writes: *The reflected sunlight pierces the deep forest.* Cheng has *Ombres retournent dans la forêt profonde.* The reader, through a note at the foot of the page, learns that *ombres retournent* — a rather forced trope — means the rays of the setting sun. And why *shadows* and not *light* or *brightness* or something similar? I wavered a great deal about translating this line. First I wrote: *Cruza el follaje el sol poniente.* (The western sun crosses the foliage.) But the poet does not speak of foliage but rather of the forest. I then tried: *Traspasa el bosque el sol poniente.* (The western sun crosses through the forest.) Somewhat better, but perhaps too energetic, too active. Next I decided to omit the verb, as Spanish allowed the ellipsis. The two syntactical blocks (*bosque profundo / luz poniente*; deep forest / western light) preserved the impersonality of the original and at the same time alluded to the silent ray of light crossing through the overgrowth.

According to Cheng, the last line means: *still — to shine — on — green — moss.* Liu says: *again — shine — green — moss — upon.* That is: the reflection is green. In his literal version Weinberger includes all of the possibilities: *to return / again — to shine / to reflect — green / blue / black — moss / lichen — above — / on (top of) / top.* In two places my version departs from the others. First: the western light *illuminates* the moss — in place of reflecting it or shining on it — because the verb *illuminate* contains both the physical aspect of the phenomenon (shining, light, clarity, brightness) and the spiritual (to illuminate understanding). Second: I say that the green reflection *ascends* or *rises* because I want to accentuate the spiritual character of the scene. The light of the western sun refers to the point of the horizon ruled by the Amida Buddha. Without trying to pin down the floating game of analogies, one might say that the western sun is the spiritual light of the paradise of the West, the cardinal point of the Amida Buddha; the solitude of the mountain and the forest is this world in which there is nobody really, though we hear the echoes of voices; and the clearing in the forest illuminated by the silent ray of light is the one who meditates and contemplates.

—OCTAVIO PAZ, 1986
(TRANS. ELIOT WEINBERGER)

POSTSCRIPT

After the publication of this essay, along with Paz's afterword, in the Mexican magazine *Vuelta*, the editors received a furious letter from a professor at the Colegio de México, charging me with nothing less than "crimes against Chinese poetry." Among those criminal acts was the "curious neglect" of "Boodberg's cedule."

The cryptic reference, I later discovered, was to *Cedules from a Berkeley Workshop in Asiatic Philology*, a series of essays privately published by Peter A. Boodberg in 1954 and 1955. Boodberg was of Russian nobility, was exiled to Manchuria and later the United States after the revolution, and became a beloved and eccentric professor of Chinese at the University of California. (Gary Snyder was one of his students.) He died in 1972.

The relevant essay, "Philology in Translation-Land," is 1½ pages long. It begins:

> Recent readings in translations of Tang quatrains have left us immersed in deep sadness in the face of the lack of philological acumen, the critical shallowness, and the self-centered irreverence towards great poetry exhibited by would-be competent writers seeming unable to resist the lures of precocious publication.

Boodberg complains that "all translators known to me (including, alas, modern Chinese and Japanese authors) betray their listless misconception of the whole poem" by failing to recognize that *shang*, usually translated as *above, on [top of], top*, can also mean, when pronounced in a different tone, *to rise* or *ascend*.

This usage is now rare, and was more common in Wang Wei's time. But for those who doubt the accuracy of poetry translated by poets rather than scholars, it should be noted that Octavio Paz, in his latest version of the poem, apparently intuitively divined this reading and translated the word as *asciende*.

Boodberg ends his "cedule" with his own version of the poem, which he calls "a still inadequate, yet philologically correct, rendition of the stanza (with due attention to grapho-syntactic overtones and enjambment)":

Deer Wattle (Hermitage)

The empty mountain: to see no men,
Barely earminded of men talking — countertones
And antistrophic lights-and-shadows incoming deeper the
    deep-treed grove
Once more to glowlight the blue-green mosses — going up
(The empty mountain . . .)

To me this sounds like Gerard Manley Hopkins on LSD, and I am grateful to the Furious Professor for sending me in search of this, the strangest of the many Weis.

[1986]

MORE WAYS

Since the writing of *Nineteen Ways* in 1979, there have been many other published translations. What follows is a sample, continuing the chronological order, of more recent versions. It is worth noting that most or all of the English-language translators were aware of the book, which was originally published in 1987. Their translations, like all re-translations, are both implicit criticisms of the previous versions of the poem (what they thought was missing, what they thought they could do better) and the results of the challenge to produce something different.

20

(A few German translations)

Günther Debon (1921–2005) was an important scholar whom some consider to be the finest German translator of classical Chinese and Japanese. A rhyming version in poetic language:

Im Hirschhagen

Am öden Berg —kein Mensch ist rings zu sehn.
Zuweilen hört man Menschenstimmen bloß.
Ein Abendstrahl dringt in den tiefen Wald.
Da liegt er leuchtend auf dem grünen Moos.

–GÜNTHER DEBON, 1988
(Debon, *Mein Haus liegt menschenfern doch nah
den Dingen. Dreitausend Jahre chinesischer Poesie*
[My House Is Far from People, Yet Close
to Things: 3000 Years of Chinese Poetry])

[*In the Deer Park*. On the deserted mountain, no one is seen around. /At times one only hears people's voices. / An evening ray penetrates into the deep forest. / It lies bright on the green moss.]

Another rhyming version that invents an explicit Chinese-style parallel (*eye / ear*) that isn't exactly in the Chinese:

61

Hirschgehege

Bergeinsamkeit, so weit das Auge reicht,
es hört allein das Ohr noch Menschen sprechen.
Den hohen Wald durchdringen Abendstrahlen,
die sich im dunklen Grün des Mooses brechen.

— VOLKER KLÖPSCH, 1991
(Klöpsch, *Der seidene Faden. Gedichte der Tang*)

[*Deer Enclosure*. Mountain solitude as far as the eye can see,
/ it is only the ear that still hears people talking. / The high
forest is penetrated by evening rays / that refract in the
dark green of the moss.]

And this, from the one book of Wang Wei's poetry available in German. It is perhaps most notable as the only translation that has no *deer*:

Am Wildgehege

Leere Berge —kein Mensch ist zu sehen,
Und dennoch hört man Menschenstimmen widerhallen.
Der Abendsonne Widerschein dringt in den tiefen Wald,
Blitzt abermals zurückgeworfen auf dem grünen Moos.

— STEPHAN SCHUHMACHER, 2009
(Wang Wei, *Jenseits der weißen Wolken*)

[*Near the Game Enclosure.* Empty mountains —no man is to be seen, / And yet one hears human voices echoing. / The evening sun's reflection enters the deep wood, / Flashes again reflected back on the green moss.]

21

Clos aux Cerfs

Montagne vide. Plus personne en vue.
Seul échos des voix résonnant au loin.
Rayon du couchant dans le bois profond:
Sur les mousses un ultime éclat: vert.

— FRANÇOIS CHENG, 1990
(Cheng, *Entre Source et Nuage: La poésie chinoise réinventée*)

[*Deer Enclosure*. Empty mountain. Not another person in sight. / Only echoes of voices resound far off. / Ray of sunset in the deep woods: / On the mosses a last gleaming: green.]

Le Clos-aux-Cerfs

Montagne déserte. Plus personne en vue
Seuls résonnent quelques échos de voix
Un rayon du couchant pénétrant le fond
Du bois: ultime éclat de la mousse, vert

— FRANÇOIS CHENG, 1996
(Cheng, *L'écriture poétique chinoise* [revised edition])

[*Deer-Enclosure*. Deserted mountain. Not another person in sight / Only resound some echoes of voices / A ray of sunlight penetrates the depths / Of the woods: last gleaming of the moss, green]

Cheng has rewritten his translation twice since his first version (#17) in 1977, the second time for a new edition of his classic *Chinese Poetic Writing*. The first version is repeated here for ease of comparison:

Clos aux cerfs

Montagne déserte. Personne n'est en vue.
Seuls, les échos des voix résonnent, au loin.
Ombres retournent dans la forêt profonde :
Dernier éclat de la mousse, vert.

— FRANÇOIS CHENG, 1977

[*Deer Enclosure*. Deserted mountain. No one in sight. / Only, the echoes of voices resound, far off. / Shadows return to the deep forest: / Last gleaming of the moss, green.]

Line 1: Cheng changes the Romantic *deserted mountain* to the Buddhist *empty mountain* and then back to the Romantic *deserted mountain*. The Buddhist *No one in sight* becomes the Romantic *Not another person (no one else) in sight*, which implies, like a painting by Caspar David Friedrich, a viewer of the mountain scene.

Line 2: He drops the hesitant commas from the 1977 version. Then he drops the *far off* (which is not in the Chinese) from 1977 and 1990, but adds *a few* echoes of voices, evoking, without saying it, the distance.

Line 3: Although he had previously noted that *returning shadows* is a trope meaning *rays of sunset*, he now abandons the *shadows* for the *rays*. The *forêt* is now a less threatening *bois*. In the 1996 version, he enjambs the line, which classical Chinese poetry never does and few translators do. (The exception in English is David Hinton [#28].)

Line 4: He goes back and forth between *last gleaming of the moss* and *last gleaming on the moss*, though the Chinese rather clearly has the sun shining *on* the moss. Whether *ultime* or *dernier*, he still insists on a *last* gleaming, which is not explicit in the original. The mysteriously hanging *green* remains, though by 1996 most of the punctuation has been dropped.

Among various other French translations, this one is noticeably different:

L'enclos du cerf

Dans la montagne vide l'homme est invisible,
Où la voix seule vient en échos.
Les ombres du couchant s'inversent dans la forêt—
Sur la mousse renaît la lumière . . .

— PATRICK CARRÉ, 1989
(Carré, *Les Saisons bleues: L'oeuvre de Wang Weï*)

[*The Deer Enclosure.* On the empty mountain man is invisible, / Where only voices come in echoes. / The shadows of the sunset invert in the forest / On the moss the light is reborn . . .)

Carré brings back the hesitant ellipsis of Bynner and Kiang (#5) and adds a dash to make the poem even more fragmentary. Invisible Man is, of course, his invention, and he creates an explicitly allegorical reading for the last line. Chinese poetry always says it without saying it, and it is unlikely that Wang Wei or any other Chinese poet would have the light *reborn*.

22

Deer Park

Nobody in sight on the empty mountain
but human voices are heard far off.
Low sun slips deep in the forest
and lights the green hanging moss.

—TONY BARNSTONE, WILLIS BARNSTONE
& XU HAIXIN, 1991
(Wang Wei, *Laughing Lost in the Mountains*)

Perhaps inspired by Kenneth Rexroth (#11), the three translators add *far off*. Undoubtedly inspired by Rexroth, their sun also *slips* into the forest. Snyder (#19) had imagined the moss that grows up the bark of a tree. Here it is apparently a kind of Spanish moss, which is not a moss and is a New World plant that didn't exist in China.

23

Deer Park

Empty hills, no man in sight—
Just echoes of the voice of men.
In the deep wood reflected light
Shines on the blue-green moss again.

— VIKRAM SETH, 1992
(Seth, *Three Chinese Poets*)

The well-known Indian novelist Vikram Seth studied classical Chinese in college. He believes that the rhyme and meter of Chinese poetry should be attempted in English translation: "The joy of poetry for me lies not so much in transcending or escaping from the so-called bonds of artifice or constraint as in using them to enhance the power of what is being said."

Unlike other formalist translations, Seth's version manages to avoid a great deal of padding to fill out the meter and rhyme. But there is something about the ABAB rhyme scheme that makes the poem seem not only trivial, but incomplete, as though it were merely the first stanza of a longer work. The closure that rhyme brings here has the opposite effect. The *voice of men*, rather than the specific *voices of men* or the abstract *voice of man*, is puzzling.

24

Deer Enclosure

On the empty mountain, seeing no one,
Only hearing the echoes of someone's voice;
Returning light enters the deep forest,
Again shining upon the green moss.

—RICHARD W. BODMAN & VICTOR MAIR, 1994
(Mair, *The Columbia Anthology of Traditional Chinese Literature*)

This translation by two Sinologists plays on a combination of gerunds and present participles. The first couplet, though perhaps too passive, neatly avoids the problem of the absence of personal pronouns in Chinese, and *no one / someone's* emphasizes the parallelism in the original. But, by the third and fourth lines, it becomes overdone. The combination of the inversion of *Again shining*— which Snyder (#19) had done—and the use of *upon* for *on* makes it sound more like premodern poeticizing than Snyder's version. Translation is always dependent on the smallest words.

25

Deer Fence

No one is seen in deserted hills,
only the echoes of speech are heard.
Sunlight cast back comes deep in the woods
and shines once again upon the green moss.

— STEPHEN OWEN, 1996

(Owen, *An Anthology of Chinese Literature: Beginnings to 1911*)

Stephen Owen is the leading American scholar of classical Chinese poetry, an unimaginably prolific translator
and author of encyclopedic critical studies. (The poem
here appears in a 1200-page anthology of poetry and
prose, entirely translated by Owen.) He oddly calls the
20-poem sequence the "Wang Stream Collection," although, in the painted scrolls that are copies of Wang's
original, it is clearly a river and not a stream. Similarly
contrarian, he writes that "Wang's quatrains are difficult
to translate, not because they present linguistic prob-
lems, but because they are so flat and plain."

In line 1, by simply adding the definite article — *the
deserted hills* — Owen could have avoided his banal gen-
erality. (Articles, unexpectedly, may be the most difficult
thing to translate in poetry.) In line 3, he glosses the
awkward construction *sunlight cast back*, claiming that it

"refers to the late afternoon sunlight which, being low in the skies, comes in under overhead obstructions and seems to cast its rays back toward the east." Quite apart from *skies* in plural and the *overhead obstructions* that, in a forest, are otherwise known as *branches*, this seems to make no sense at all. The rays of a setting sun obviously head in an eastward direction. That the rays are heading "back" to the east and the rising sun is an extrapolation of cyclical time far greater than the return of the sunlight to the forest floor. It's hard to say line 4's *once again upon* without stammering.

26

Deer Park

No sign of men on the empty mountain,
only faint echoes from below.

Refracted light enters the forest,
shining through green moss above.

— SAM HAMILL, 2000
(Hamill, *Crossing the Yellow River*)

Hamill, a poet with some knowledge of Chinese, follows
Rexroth (#11) in reimagining the scene. The echoes are
now *faint* and come *from below*, neither of which are in the
Chinese. There is a difference between *not seeing people*
and *no sign of men*. Is this really an untouched wilderness?
Judging from (the copies of) Wang's scroll painting, and
the fact that the deer are enclosed, it is not.

Hamill is the first in English to use *refracted* for the
light—Klöpsch (#20) has *brechen*—which is lovely, but
does not indicate that it is sunset (and the word, of course,
is a product of Western science long after Wang's time).
Like Snyder (#19), he places the moss *above*, but by having
the light *shining through* the moss, he runs into the same
problem as the Barnstones and Xu (#22): wrong moss.

Apart from Debon in German (#20), Hamill is the first to employ the form of the original, known as *jueju* (*chüeh-chü*), which unhelpfully translates as *broken-off lines*. (Even the formalist Seth doesn't follow the form.) The *jueju*, which became popular in the Tang Dynasty, is a four-line poem with five characters per line, made up of two couplets. The couplets often, but not always, exhibit some kind of parallelism (in this poem, *not see people / hear people,* and the words for *return* at the beginning of both lines 3 and 4). Since it is composed of two discrete couplets, each a syntactical unit, it is not exactly a quatrain in the Western sense — Western quatrains have much more flexibility. Yet most translators present *jueju* poems as quatrains.

27

Deer Park

The mountain is empty, no man can be seen.
but the echo of human sounds is heard.
Returning sunlight, entering the deep forest,
shines again on green moss, above.

— ARTHUR SZE, 2001
(Sze, *The Silk Dragon*)

The Chinese-American poet Arthur Sze follows Snyder (#19) in translating both meanings of *xiang* (Snyder: *human sounds and echoes*, Sze: *the echo of human sounds*). And, like Snyder, he places the moss *above*.

In an interesting essay, "The Wang River Sequence, A Prospectus" (included in *Civil Disobediences*, edited by Anne Waldman & Lisa Birman), Sze connects this poem to a later one in the sequence, "Bamboo Grove," which he translates as:

I sit alone in the secluded bamboo grove
and play the zither and whistle along.
In the deep forest no one knows,
  the bright moon comes to shine on me.

The moonlight coming into the forest to shine on the poet is the twin of the late sunlight shining again on the moss. "In a sense," Sze writes, "the green moss may be the poet's mind."

28

Deer Park

No one seen. In empty mountains,
hints of drifting voice, no more.

Entering these deep woods, late sunlight ablaze on green moss, rising.

— DAVID HINTON, 2002
(Hinton, Mountain Home)

Deer Park

No one seen. Among empty mountains,
hints of drifting voice, faint, no more.

Entering these deep woods, late sunlight
flares on green moss again, and rises.

— DAVID HINTON, 2006
(Hinton, The Selected Poems of Wang Wei)

Hinton is, after Burton Watson (#12), the next in the
lineage of literary Sinologists — that is, scholars whose
work brings something into English-language literature

and is not merely a window into the original. One of his innovations is to enjamb the lines — which classical Chinese never does — as a way of giving a sense of the density of the classical poems. He also consistently translates *jueju* poems into couplets, though sometimes enjambing across them.

After translating the poem for an anthology of Chinese mountain poems, he revised it a few years later for a selection of Wang Wei. (With its infinite number of possible combinations, a translation is never finished.) These versions are quite consciously written with an awareness of previous versions and, very curiously, Hinton has picked up a few things from an otherwise dismal translation, Chang & Walmsley (#8). They somewhat pointlessly inverted the order of the couplets; Hinton transposes the images in the first line. (Translations of poetry will sometimes not follow the order of the images. This breaks no inflexible rule, but is rarely done well.) By beginning with the mysterious or dramatic *No one seen*, it almost becomes a different poem. And then Hinton transforms C & W's banal *Yet faint voices drift on the air* into an almost mimetic *hints of drifting voice, faint, no more*. In line 4, the light presumably *rises* as the sun sets.

In an extended Chan (Zen) Buddhist analysis of the poem, in his introduction to the *Selected Poems*, Hinton writes that Chinese poetry itself, with its absence of "prepositions and conjunctions, verb tenses, and very often subjects" embodies *wu*, the emptiness of nonbeing. "You mentally fill in the grammatical emptiness, and yet it always remains emptiness, and this means participating in the silence of an empty mind as the boundaries of its true, wordless form."

Moreover, this poem "begins with perception emptied of a perceiver (the absent subject), but is deepened by the fact that it is perception reduced to the very edge of emptiness: rather than people being seen, there is the absence of people being seen; and, in the second line, only the faintest hint of voice is heard, a virtual absence of voice."

A translation of, say, a poem into English is a kind of palimpsest. It is not a poem in English, as it will always be read as a translation: a text written on top of another text. Yet it is appreciated (or not appreciated) in the same ways we respond to an original poem: in awe at the delicacy and intricacy of its manipulation of the language, or disappointed by its clunkiness.

29

Deer Park

Empty mountain, none to be seen.
Listen close and all you'll hear's
the birdsong sound of human language.
Sun's come into this deep grove,
beginning again, it writes on gray-green lichen, upon stone.

— J. P. SEATON, 2006
(Seaton, *The Shambhala Anthology of Chinese Poetry*)

The Sinologist J. P. Seaton, who had previously translated the poem for the English version of François Cheng's *Chinese Poetic Writing* (#17), returns with a strangely amplified rendition. Some of the additions are explained in an essay he wrote, "Once More on the Empty Mountain," included in *The Poem Behind the Poem: Translating Asian Poetry*, edited by Frank Stewart (2004). Thus *the birdsong sound of human language* for the single word *sound / echo* is somewhat explained because the Chinese word combines the characters for *a musical tone*—which Seaton says was previously *a man singing*—and *countryside*. He writes: "With a little humility, humans may hear their own tongues on the level of birdsong: as simple notes in the complex music of the outdoors." The second line expands Snyder's simple *hear* (#19), but *Listen close and all you'll hear's* is a demonstration that, sometimes, accurate "real speech" is no improvement on often-maligned "literary language."

In the enigmatic fourth line, the italicized *beginning again*, according to Seaton's essay, is meant to refer to Hexagram 24 of the *I Ching,* called *Fu* (Return), which is also the first character in the line. *Fu* is a common word, and it's hardly certain that Wang is referring to the hexagram. Are the italics supposed to indicate that this is what the sun is writing on the lichen or the stone (or both)? Why is it writing *on lichen, upon stone*? In any event, the pathetic fallacy is bizarre: contrary to Derrida, not everything is writing.

[2016]

POSTSCRIPT

In 1989, two years after the US publication of *Nineteen Ways* by a small literary publisher, I received a book from Mexico: *Para leer Nineteen Ways of Looking at Wang Wei* [How to Read *Nineteen Ways*...], written by none other than the Furious Professor, and privately published at his own expense.

The Professor's book, much longer than my own, is almost a line-by-line analysis of my text, filled with violent denunciations and character assassinations. Its most entertaining moment occurs when he must concede that he actually agrees with me on some small point: "Almost nobody is perpetually totally mistaken, and here, at last, Mr. Weinberger hits the nail on the head." The book ends with a note that he is now working on a study of another of my essays on Chinese poetry—though unfortunately this has yet to materialize.

Some years later, after a reading I gave in Mexico City, a small middle-aged man with the expression of a mouse in a barn fire came scurrying over to me. "Hello, I'm the Furious Professor," he said, referring to himself by my epithet rather than his own name, "and I wanted to give you this." He handed me a manilla envelope.

"What's this? Another attack on me?"

"What else? . . . But I wanted to thank you. I was asked to deliver this paper at a conference in Hawaii. I had a wonderful time, and all thanks to you!" Before I could reply, he had disappeared into the crowd.

Naturally I couldn't wait to read his latest. It turned out to be a critical study, written in English, of some modern Chinese translations of a classical Chinese poem. Although this is a subject I have never written about—in fact, know nothing about—the Professor periodically interrupted his discussion for my supposed response: "This incorporates a number of features dear to Weinberger's heart" or "It is not difficult to imagine the scandalized cries of alarm on the part of Weinberger and his colleagues." (An enemy force, I had now become a group.)

Surely the Furious Professor is the purest form of literary critic: a man who devotes his life to demolishing the work of a writer no one else knows. Clearly he is the only reader who truly needs me. But, lounging on the beaches of Hawaii, does he ever have a moment of panic: the thought that I, in the freezing New York winter, might, just to spite him, stop typing?

[2016]